ONE BRANCH

Stuart Bartow

ONE BRANCH

ISBN 978-1-947271-47-0

Red Moon Press
PO Box 2461
Winchester VA
22604-1661 USA
www.redmoonpress.com

Cover photo: Marcelo Silva

first printing

ONE BRANCH

open all night
the path
into the woods

owl's skull
no wonder
their calls so strange

last night's dreams
scarecrows
and mist

winter nights near the woodstove
cats sprawled
across my table

released
from the screech owl's whinny
the forest

the mountains of Pluto
something far away
in all of us

the bear in my window   winter stars

blizzard night
above it all
stars

⚱ FABLE

When I first moved to the house near the marsh, a neighbor told me of a white stag who lived in the swamp. Hunters stalked the stag for years, but were never able to kill him. Perhaps the marsh was impenetrable, or the stag too wily, or just lucky. Would the story have moved me if *Moby Dick* had never been written? The whale, like the stag, is the real hero. And where, after all, do these beings arise from, but from the imagination, which is an ocean.

> frozen marsh
> who
> is dreaming whom

antenna still over the roof
those old shows
deep space

flying fish over snow drifts   snow buntings

last night's snow
storm star
charts on the windows

winter wind tears
the spider webs   my house
flies away

too sleepy to get up
the haiku
vanishes

dashboard Yoda
shielding us
from the snowstorm's force

in the forgotten graveyard   crow funeral

clothing drop off

my brother's cowboy boots

🕯 MIGRATION

My sister's body, overdosed, found in an abandoned house. A couple days after the funeral I was driving my 15-year-old niece to her friend's house when she asked if I thought her mother would go to hell. No. I replied, she'll go to heaven, but she'll have to stand in line for a long time.

> a wobbly V of geese
> flying
> in the wrong direction

heaven in a wild flower
a bumblebee
emerges

geese waking me before dawn
how many souls
are you carrying south

full moon over my house
just as bright
as over McMansions

winter night
shoveling stars
off the roof

Einstein first predicted the existence of black holes decades before astrophysicists confirmed their reality, though no one can see one. We can photograph them, but we really only imagine event horizons, the region just before matter disappears into a black hole. Scientists have also traced the beginning of the universe up to a micro-second, that first trillionth of a second, the singularity, unreachable. Maybe the universe began as a black hole that exploded, which would mean that time and space are infinite, never ending, or once ending, beginning over and over again whenever a black hole reaches its singularity point, no larger than a poppy seed.

> after the movie
> we stand in the rain wondering
> what happens next

honeybees' hive
star frequencies
only they can hear

bristling stars
the hives of heaven
awake

dream last night
embracing a strange woman
light snowfall

into thin air

the hundred year old catalpa
for a driveway

sculpture park
the best piece
someone's snowman

someone whistling
in the diner's kitchen
if I only had a brain

imagining Pluto
the wind
at 4 a.m.

winter wood
so that's where
the songs were hidden

⚘ ONE BRANCH

Here in the northern Taconics, between the Adirondacks and Green Mountains, winter is the most prevalent season. Even in summer people like me are preparing for winter, filling our woodsheds, cleaning our woodstoves, repairing storm doors. Yesterday, February 23rd, the thermometer on the back porch reached 71 degrees Fahrenheit, shattering old records. Today, 76 degrees. A woman at the post office told me that December an old apple tree in her yard blossomed. But only one branch.

> waking at 4 a.m.
> a blizzard
> of white moths

troubled dreams
all night
into birdsong

carrying flower pots out
of the dark shed
surprising the spiders

old factory
feral cats
perched in the windows

mantids in the mail
the mad gardener
in me

♪ TRANSLATION

Carpenter ants like to excavate their nests in dying trees, but sometimes they nest in walls and, at night, you might hear them rustling like aluminum foil being crumpled. Finding no other function for the sound, entomologists theorize they are communicating. Could they be chattering, singing, or chanting?

> radio waves
> who to unscramble the songs
> we send into space

from my porch
a distant star
strange to have two homes

forgotten where
the crocuses were planted

hocus pocus

lightning storm no lights no radio   katydids

moon in the stream
my lure vanishes
into the sea of tranquility

the only words I catch
from her morning song
bese, sombra, sueno

in the marsh pond
I watch the moon bathing
her naked ghost

mating in flight darning needles   don't mind me

in the monarch's brain
Mexico Maine
and everywhere in between

in my garden
dynasties
of pharaoh ants

Pleiades

Boys in the house are playing video games, while I go outside to the marsh where hundreds of fireflies blink their green lights in a maze of drifting constellations. Some futurists believe the human race may eventually split into different species: those who will remain grounded in the earth, and those who will morph into cyberspace where they will dwell in worlds of their own.

not one soul tonight
fireflies
mimic the Pleiades

half-buried bottle
ants' palace
through a glass darkly

night fishing
my lure lost
in the stars

cattail marsh
nobody knows
but flycatchers and me

who will watch
when I leave

morning star

spring peepers
the marsh will be a baritone
later

Fermi's paradox
the stars
too far to hear

ATAVISM

Often when I am forest hiking I will see in the distance what looks to be a person, standing still or oddly moving in the breeze. But as I approach, vision clarifies and it turns out to be a tree, stump, or shrub. So reason dominates imagination, regrettably, at times. What's interesting is that it's never the reverse. I never see what I thought to be a sapling turn into a human. Maybe an old atavism is at work. In classical myth people change into trees, birds, fountains, stars, but never a stream, spider, deer, or bush into a human. Are there rules or patterns that the imagination is always destined to obey, as in physics, where time can move only in one direction, as far as we know?

trying
to get close enough
the checkerspot's face

last week's haircut
is that me
in the phoebe's nest

fireflies in the marsh
the stars also
wandering

a picture-book garden
but mine
has wild bees

summer woolly bears
as if a caterpillar's coat
could forecast cold

chickadees in the mailbox
news
from the sky

one note only   bullfrogs' fugue

afterwards
he even waters
the plastic flowers

latest map
of the universe
dandelion seeds

driving back roads
more moths
than imagination's calculus

darners mating   in flight

                          la vida loca

long twig
round hole
wren physics

𝍓 ROMANIA

At the end of the dream, most of which I don't remember, a man with long hair and a beard tells me that the poet John Donne is buried in Romania. I'd always understood Donne to be entombed in Westminster Abbey. Could he have been a vampire? In the lone picture the world has of him, he does look like one.

daybreak
chickadees nesting
in the bluebird house

road rescuing
        the turtle
            pees on me

windy night
        the moon slips
                out of her negligee

no more working
in the woodshed

jays' nest

on the map it seemed
so much larger
      mountain pond

breaking the day
        dream a flock
                of sparrows

five red admirals
in the garden
mission accomplished

1930's first baseman's mitt
summers buried
in the leather

KIDS FOR SALE
away in a field
stray goats

nearing the pond
just as the peepers
                    stop

peony buds
ants
trying to open the doors

lightning bugs
in the old graveyard
heaven   sort of

between the tires
and the shopping carts   casting   for trout

garden gnomes

everywhere
Buddha's avatars

bulrush marsh
near the ruined factory
peepers
on the graveyard shift

old farm gone
to meadow
brown butterflies grazing

⚱ NOTHING

The sign on the door at the end of the bar read, *There is Nothing Behind this Door*. Strange. There has to be something behind the door: a brick wall, a dead-end alley, a mineshaft, a closet, another door, the infinite void (if such a space exists). But is an infinite void some thing? There are voids between galaxies, but even those vast spaces have subatomic particles. Then there is dark energy, dark matter, and the universe filled with galaxies, 170 billion, roughly. Stars, planets, asteroid belts, nebulae.

> drifting clouds all night
> suddenly
> one star

sugar ants roam
the counter   she asks
do ants dream

toadflax fields
without
the
toads

hovering my red shirt
the hummingbird decides
not to taste me

before the lawnmower grasshopper stampede

driving by my old house
the blackberry patch
escaping the fence

after the concert a cicada's solo

neglected garden
cabbage whites spinning helixes
not hearts

October spiderlings
where will you go
for winter

rushing through the pages
the wind
wants an ending

woolly bears hurrying
slowly
October migration

Halloween night
a witch rings
my dead doorbell

psychic reading
someone trying to trap me

phone call from an ex

wind in the reeds
an almost human
whisper

she leaves again
a doe
disappearing into the woods

the far side of the moon
everything
we never found

night wind
dead languages
through the trees

her first map of the States
Venus
not Kansas

just before dawn
something dark
moving across the yard

warm autumn night
cricket song
her breathing

tired of reading
the book of stars
opens

fall's return
the scarf she gave me
lift's lightly

crickets this cool night
the window
stays open

3:00 a.m.
the wind changes
her song

The author thanks the editors of the following publications where some of these haiku and haibun first appeared:

Acorn: A Journal of Contemporary Haiku; Akitsu Quarterly; Haiku Society of America Members' Anthology, 2017 and 2018; *The Heron's Nest; Modern Haiku; New England Letters; Shamrock: Journal of the Irish Haiku Society; Bottle Rockets; Haibun Today; Contemporary Haibun Online; Frogpond; Bones: A Haiku Journal; Failed Haiku.*

Thanks also to the Adirondack Center for Writing for a writer's residency where some of these haiku were made, Jim Kacian for his editorial acumen and creative book design, and to my consort Barbara Ungar for her editorial suggestions.

⚡ STUART BARTOW teaches writing and literature a SUNY (State University of New York) Adirondack. He is chair of the Battenkill Conservancy, an environmental group working at the New York-Vermont border. His prose work, *Teaching Trout to Talk: the Zen of Small Stream Fly Fishing*, received the 2014 best book of non-fiction award from the Adirondack Center for Writing. He has previously published seven books of poetry, including his first collection of haiku, *quaking marsh* (Red Moon Press, 2017). ONE BRANCH is his second.